D1199537

IT'S NEVER TOO LATE

DALLAS CLAYTON

Amy Einhorn Books

Published by G. P. Putnam's Sons

a member of Penguin Group (USA)

New York

AMY EINHORN BOOKS
Published by G. P. Putnam's Sons
Publishers Since 1838
Published by the Penguin Group
Penguin Group (USA) LLC
375 Hudson Street
New York, New York 10014

USA · Canada · UK · Ireland · Australia
New Zealand · India · South Africa · China

penguin.com
A Penguin Random House Company

Copyright © 2013 by Dallas Clayton
Penguin supports copyright. Copyright fuels creativity, encourages diverse voices,
promotes free speech, and creates a vibrant culture. Thank you for buying an authorized
edition of this book and for complying with copyright laws by not reproducing, scanning,
or distributing any part of it in any form without permission. You are supporting
writers and allowing Penguin to continue to publish books for every reader.

"Amy Einhorn Books" and the "ae" logo are registered trademarks
belonging to Penguin Group (USA) LLC

Library of Congress Cataloging-in-Publication Data

Clayton, Dallas.
It's never too late / Dallas Clayton.
p.   cm.
ISBN 978-0-399-16308-1
1. Self-esteem.   2. Mind and body.   I. Title.   II. Title: It is never too late.
BF697.5.S46C537   2013   2013015508
158.1—dc23

Printed in the United States of America
1   3   5   7   9   10   8   6   4   2

Book design by Meighan Cavanaugh

For all the grown-ups

If today was the day
that it all came crashing,
with thunderclaps
and lightning flashing,

how would you feel?
Where would you stand?
Who would you want
to hold your hand?

What would you care
of bills and debt?
Or opinions of people
you'd never met?

What would you think
of the laundry pile?
Or the kitchen sink?
Or the bathroom tile?

What would you do
with those final hours?
Would you lie in the grass?
Would you smell the flowers?

Would you wear a dress?
Would you sing a song?
Would you make a mess?
Would you right a wrong?

Would you set your alarm
or straighten your bed?
Or hug your cat
and dog instead?

Would you scream and yell
or laugh and cry?
Would you call your friends
to say good-bye?

And what if today
just kept on going,
and day after day
there was no way of knowing
when it would end
or how it would be?

Would you still live each hour
like a bird in a tree?

'Cause the truth
is that nobody knows what to say
when the air gets cold
and the sky turns gray.

And the truth
is that nobody has all the answers,
and everyone's singers
and everyone's dancers.

And everyone's sink
gets all full of dishes,
and everyone's heart
gets all full of wishes.

And everyone's mind
gets all full of mess,
and we all read the signs,
and we all try our best.

But it's never too late
to say that you care,
to call up a friend
you wish was still there.

And it's never too late
to start something new,
to do all those things
you've been longing to do.

Because this is your life,
this moment right now.
As you read this
the world is just spinning around.

And each moment
is a moment that's ticking away.
So what will you do?
And what will you say?

And what will you be?
And what will you give?
And what will you make
of these moments you live?

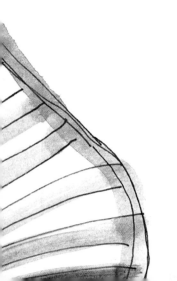

Because you could be anything,
and you could be all,
and you could be out there
just having a ball.

And you could be failing
and trying again,
and you could be changing
the way it'll end.

And you could be bigger,
and you could be better,
and you could mend hearts
just by writing a letter,

just by telling a story
or sharing a smile,
or sitting and talking
and laughing awhile.

And all the traffic
and all the bills
and all the pressure
and all the ills,

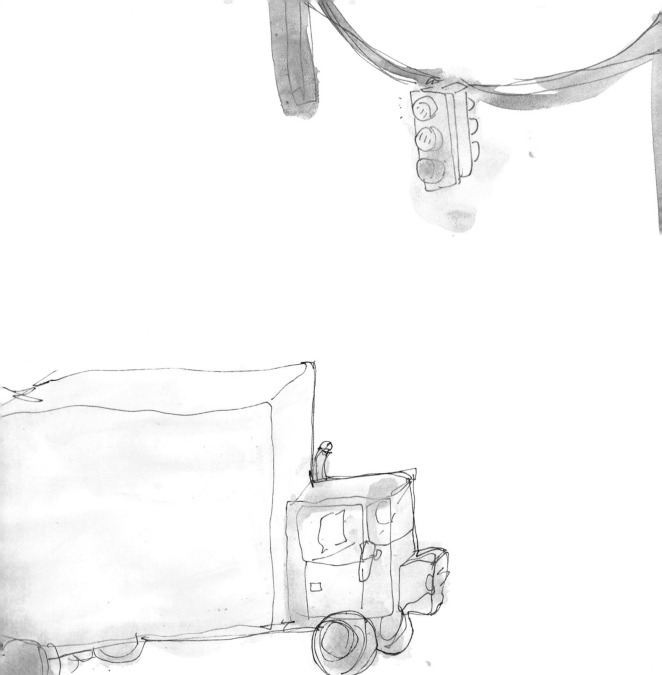

well, those will keep coming;
of this I am certain.
But in those last moments
when you pull back the curtain,
it's the love you'll remember,
that you gave and you got,

and the times you were certain,
and the times you were not,

and the times you were open,
and the times that you had
when you felt like a child
or you hugged like a dad

or you smiled like a mom
or you cried like forever.
Those are the moments
you're going to remember.

So go and collect them,
create them and share,
find them and pull them
right out of the air,
and shape them and give them
to others who care.

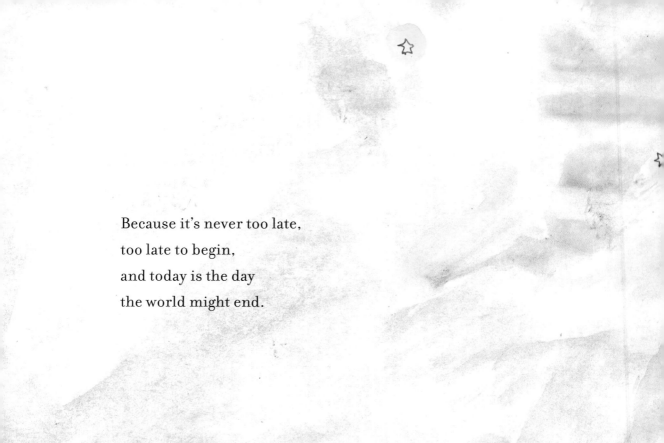

Because it's never too late,
too late to begin,
and today is the day
the world might end.

And today is the day
the world might start,
so live it and love it
with all of your heart.

ABOUT THE AUTHOR

Called "the New Dr. Seuss," Dallas Clayton is known for his vivid use of colors, powerful themes, and magical wordplay. Clayton makes his home in Los Angeles, but can be found touring the world, spreading his message of the importance of following your dreams. *It's Never Too Late* is his first adult book.